AUNT TABITHA'S

GIFT

BY CAROL KRUEGER

ILLUSTRATED BY JOSH WATENE

AUNT TABITHA'S GIFT

"I've got all A's again!" said Matthew, waving his report card.

"I haven't," said Anna. "I never do as well as you, Matthew."

"Well, it's just bad luck that you have to compete with a brother who's a genius!" grinned Matthew.

"Genius!" said Mum. "Hmmm! Today we're going to visit a real genius – Aunt Tabitha."

"I don't want to visit her!" said Matthew.

"You could open up those genius ears and learn something," said Mum. "She's written heaps of books about spiders and insects. She's a great expert."

"And she's weird," said Matthew.

"I like her," said Anna.

CLARIFY:
weird

A	strange
B	serious
C	ordinary

A, B or C?

3

That afternoon, they drove to Aunt Tabitha's house. Its little window eyes seemed to glare at them. Ivy climbed up the side and strangled the chimney.

"This house should be used in a horror movie," said Matthew. "And Aunt Tabitha should star in the movie!"

"Matthew!" Mum growled.

They walked up the broken path. Weeds pushed their way through their concrete prison. Untrimmed bushes ran wild. Then they heard a loud howl.

"Oh, no! She's probably got a pet wolf now!" groaned Matthew.

Anna shivered, even though she knew . . .

Matthew was just winding her up.

METAPHOR:

A metaphor creates a mind picture in which one thing is described as if it were actually that thing.

Can you find a metaphor

The creaky front door opened and Aunt Tabitha stood there smiling. Beside her stood a huge dog. He was snarling.

His teeth looked like a row of sharp, wet knives.

"This is my friend's dog, Sweetie," said Aunt Tabitha. "I'm babysitting him for the weekend. Don't worry, he doesn't bite."

Aunt Tabitha looked like an old willow branch. She was tall and graceful and wrinkled with years.

"Come in," she said.

SIMILE:

A simile is a group of words that helps the reader draw a mind picture. It uses the words "like" or "as" to make a comparison.

Can you find a simile

Anna spent the next two hours looking at Aunt Tabitha's collection of dolls and spoons while Matthew sulked. She looked excitedly at Aunt Tabitha's dusty books while Matthew sneezed.

Finally, Aunt Tabitha took them up to the attic and showed them a large glass case. Inside was an enormous spider.

"He's awesome!" said Anna.

"He's gross!" said Matthew.

"He's called Tiberius," said Aunt Tabitha. "He's a goliath tarantula."

"Well, I think he's awful!" said Matthew, and on the way home, he only stopped complaining to eat a burger and some fries.

INFERENCE:

What can you infer from Matthew's behaviour about the way he felt about the visit to Aunt Tabitha?

. . . . he's a goliath tarantula

Months went by. Matthew won the school speech competition, the chess championship and scored the winning goal at soccer, and Aunt Tabitha died. She was ninety-three. The day after the funeral, the phone rang.

"It'll be for Matthew," said Anna. "Nobody ever bothers about me."

"Well it's not my fault I'm so popular!" Matthew grinned.

Mum answered the phone and then she smiled. "Aunt Tabitha left something in her will for Anna."

"What about me?" asked Matthew.

"No – just for Anna," Mum said.

CHARACTER PROFILE:

Which words best describe the
character of Matthew?

brave

shy

talented

clever

confident

show-off

On the way to the lawyer's office, Matthew fumed and Anna dreamed. She imagined having the beautiful dolls or the diamond necklace, or maybe even the quaint clock.

When the lawyer read out her name, Anna held her breath and closed her eyes.

"I leave to my great niece, Anna Martin – my tarantula, Tiberius."

Anna gasped.

Matthew burst out laughing.

. . . . my tarantula, Tiberius

Tiberius came home in his glass case. He rested in Anna's room while Matthew was sent to catch flies for his lunch.

Anna looked at Tiberius. She put her hand gently into the case and stroked his black furry body. Tiberius slowly crept onto her hand, and then he climbed up her arm. It felt like thousands of tiny feathers softly tickling her skin. Anna knew that Tiberius trusted her.

The next day, she took him to school. She showed him at assembly. The teachers stared in astonishment. At lunchtime, the newspaper took photos of Anna with Tiberius on her face. After that the phone didn't stop ringing.

SIMILE:

Can you find a simile?

See page 7 for a clue!

... thousands of tiny feathers

Everybody wanted Anna to come and talk about Tiberius. She went to a kindergarten, four schools and she was on T.V. Nobody was even interested in the science competition that Matthew won.

Then Anna realised that she wasn't shy any more. She could talk to people now as easily as Matthew could. She was making lots of new friends. She even had enough courage to enter a singing competition at the mall.

One day, Mum drove Anna and Tiberius to the city library. Anna was giving a talk, and they were running late. The lights seemed to have a spell on them. They kept turning red. Then the car got stuck behind an old bus. Finally, they arrived at the library. "We'll run in and tell them we're here," said Mum, "and then we'll come back and lock up."

INFERENCE:

What can you infer about Anna's confidence since she started looking after Tiberius?

The library was packed with people waiting to see Tiberius. "We're here," said Mum breathlessly.

"Where is the spider?" someone said.

Anna's cheeks went red. "He is in the car," she said. "I forgot to bring him in."

I forgot to bring him in.

Anna and her mother raced out to the carpark. Suddenly they stopped in their tracks. Someone had stolen the car and was driving it out of the carpark. Anna's heart was pounding. She was too frightened to move. Her breath was coming out in strange little gasps. She tried to stop the tears from rolling down her cheeks, but they spilled over like water over a dam.

Mum gave a hair-raising screech. "Stop!" she yelled. "That's our car!"

A security guard rushed over.

"Someone's got my car!" shouted Mum.

Mum and Anna looked at each other in shock as the security guard rang the police.

"Will we ever get our car back?" asked Anna. She shivered with anxiety. "He has got my spider, Tiberius!"

"Don't worry!" said the security man. "Some car thieves are quite cunning but the police have clever ways to track them."

ACTION AND RESPONSE

ACTION	RESPONSE
Anna's heart was pounding	She was too frightened to move
Mum screeched	?

Slowly Anna and her mother walked back into the library. It was so quiet inside that Anna could hear the library clock ticking. It seemed to beat in time with her heart. "Tiberius is gone! Someone just stole our car," said Mum.

"He's been abducted," said a small boy.

Anna froze inside; then she felt the tears well up again. They slid down her face and ran, wet and salty, into her mouth.

"Tiberius will be OK. You'll get him back," said Mum. "Who would want a big black spider for a pet!"

Just then, the security guard came into the library. He smiled at Anna and Mum. "The police have found your car but . . .," he said, "it's been in an accident and they need Anna's help."

EMOTIONS:

Which words best describe how Anna might be feeling?

calm   annoyed   shocked

panicky   excited   desperate

afraid   frightened   happy

Anna and Mum followed the security man back to his car and they drove through the city streets. Then they saw their car – corralled by police cars, like a beast at a roundup.

"I think we need a hand here," said one of the police officers.

Anna and Mum hurried toward the car. Slumped down in the front seat was the car thief. Tiberius strutted across the thief's face like a soldier on parade. Up and down, up and down . . .

The thief was snivelling loudly. "I hate these things! Get me out of here!"

"I'm not too fond of these spiders," said the officer. "I don't think it's part of our job to handle large spiders," said another officer.

CLARIFY:
corralled

A	picked up
B	penned
C	stopped

A, B or C?

. . . I hate these things!

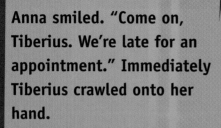

Anna smiled. "Come on, Tiberius. We're late for an appointment." Immediately Tiberius crawled onto her hand.

"He's a smart spider," said one of the officers. "We've been trying to catch this thief for ages and Tiberius has caught him in a few minutes."

The next day Anna and Tiberius were in the paper again – on the front page. Everyone was pleased. Well – everyone except Matthew.

SUMMARY:

What key points would you include in a summary of *Aunt Tabitha's Gift*?

- Anna's brother was clever and popular.
- Anna was left a spider in Aunt Tabitha's will.
- Anna could hold the spider in her hand and stroke his body.
- Everybody wanted Anna to talk about the spider.
- Anna had to talk at the library.
- A thief stole the car with the spider in it.
- The thief was scared of the spider.
- The police were pleased the spider helped them catch the car thief.

THINK ABOUT THE TEXT

What connections can you make to the emotions, situations or characters of *Aunt Tabitha's Gift*?

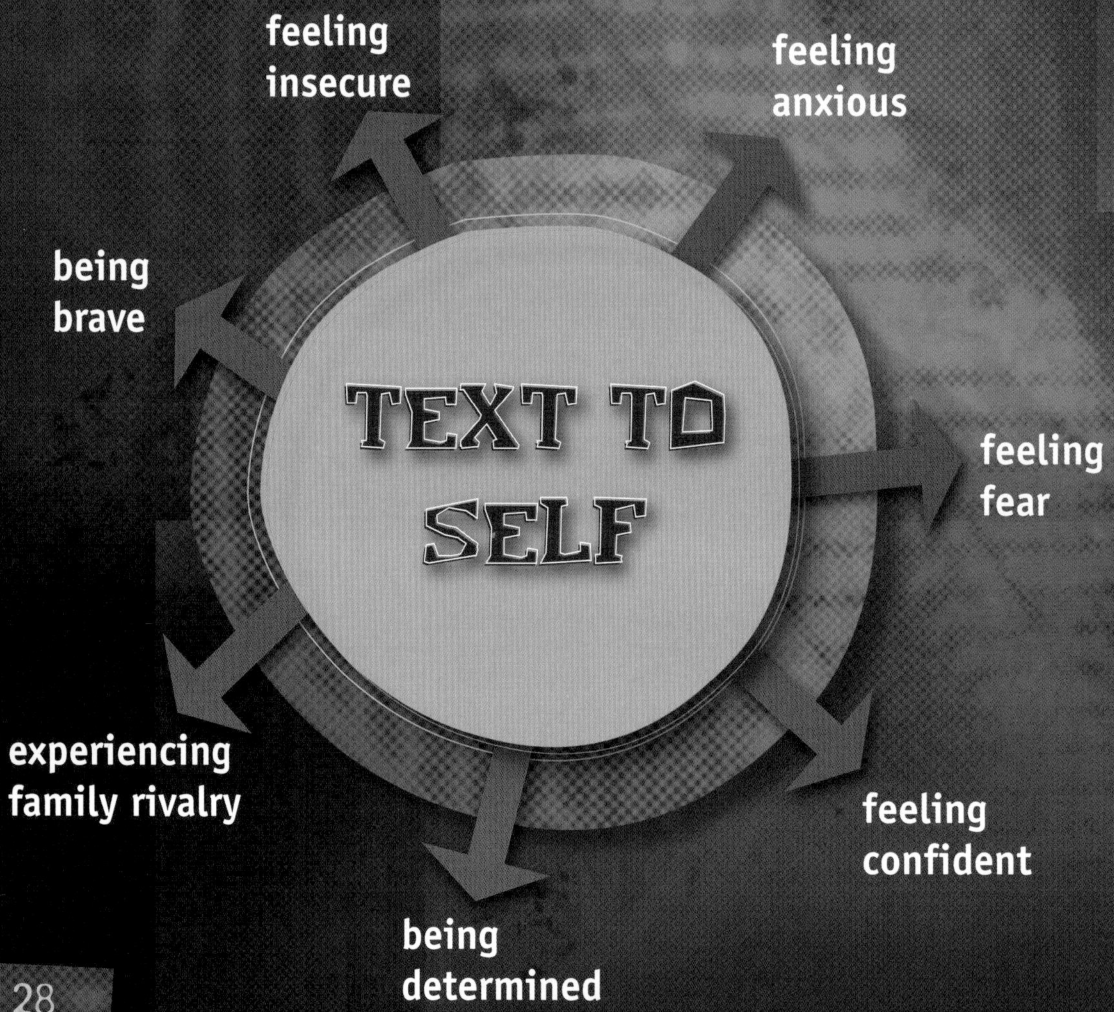

feeling insecure

feeling anxious

being brave

TEXT TO SELF

feeling fear

experiencing family rivalry

feeling confident

being determined

TEXT TO TEXT

Talk about other stories you may have read that have similar features. Compare the stories.

TEXT TO WORLD

Talk about situations in the world that might connect to elements in the story.

PLANNING A NARRATIVE

1 Decide on a storyline that has an introduction, a problem and a solution

INTRODUCTION:
Matthew, Anna and Mum visit Aunt Tabitha, who dies a few months later, and leaves Anna a tarantula in her will.

PROBLEM:
Anna takes her tarantula to the library to give a talk, but the car gets stolen with the tarantula in it.

SOLUTION:
The tarantula frightens the car thief, resulting in his arrest, and Anna gets her tarantula back.

2 Think about the characters and how they will think, feel and act

Anna

Aunt Tabitha

Matthew

Mum

3 Decide on the setting

Location

SETTING

Time

Atmosphere

4 Think about events in order of sequence

Aunt Tabitha shows Anna her tarantula, Tiberius.

Aunt Tabitha leaves Tiberius to Anna in her will.

NARRATIVES USUALLY . . .

have an introduction that quickly tells:

- who the story is about
- where the story is set
- when the story happened

have a problem that creates excitement and makes the reader want to read on to find out how the problem is solved

create an emotional response within the reader

include description and dialogue

create mood and tension

include characters, setting and mood that are connected to create a believable storyline